A LADYBIRD 'EASY-READING' BOOK

The story of
FOOTBALL

by V. SOUTHGATE, M.A., B.Com.
with illustrations by JACK MATTHEW

Publishers: Wills & Hepworth Ltd   Loughborough
First published 1964   ©   Printed in England

THE STORY OF FOOTBALL

Nearly all boys like to play football. Whenever a few boys are playing together, some of them are sure to be kicking a ball about. They do this whether they are in a garden or yard, in the street, in parks or fields, or on the beach.

If there are no proper goal-posts, boys use tin cans, piles of stones, or boys' jackets. If they do not have a proper football, they will kick a big rubber ball, a small ball, or even a stone.

4

F.A. Challenge Cup Finalists
1950 - 1970

Winners	*Opponents*
1950 Arsenal	Liverpool
1951 Newcastle United	Blackpool
1952 Newcastle United	Arsenal
1953 Blackpool	Bolton Wanderers
1954 West Bromwich Albion	Preston North End
1955 Newcastle United	Manchester City
1956 Manchester City	Birmingham City
1957 Aston Villa	Manchester United
1958 Bolton Wanderers	Manchester United
1959 Nottingham Forest	Luton
1960 Wolverhampton Wanderers	Blackburn Rovers
1961 Tottenham Hotspur	Leicester City
1962 Tottenham Hotspur	Burnley
1963 Manchester United	Leicester City
1964 West Ham United	Preston North End
1965 Liverpool	Leeds United
1966 Everton	Sheffield Wednesday
1967 Tottenham Hotspur	Chelsea
1968 West Bromwich Albion	Everton
1969 Manchester City	Leicester City
1970 Chelsea	Leeds United

Series 606C

Here is a book that will interest every boy, and encourage even the most reluctant young reader to get extra reading practice.

With simple text and superb full-colour illustrations, it tells the story of Football from the days when hundreds of men took part in one game to the present day Cup Finals.

Long ago men used to play football in the village streets. Hundreds of men played in one game at the same time.

The bladder of an animal was blown up to make a ball. This ball was kicked or punched or carried by the men. All the men tried to get at the ball at the same time.

The game used to become very rough. Men's hats and coats were often torn in the struggle to get at the ball. Often men's arms or legs were broken.

Every year, on Shrove Tuesday, a game of football was played in a town called Chester. The shoe-makers used to make a new leather ball and give it to the drapers in the town.

Then the drapers played football with the new ball through the streets of the town. One goal was at one end of the town and the other goal was at the other end of the town.

Hundreds of men played in the game. There was only one rule, to get the ball into the opponent's goal. It did not matter how this was done or who was hurt in the struggle.

Often, on Shrove Tuesday, there were games between two villages. The goals were three or four miles apart. There were often fields, hedges, ditches and streams between the two goals.

All the men in the two villages took part in the game. By the end of the game they were usually covered with mud and dirt. Many of the men fell into the streams and ditches and their clothes became wet.

Some of the men were injured because they had fallen down. Others were injured because they had been kicked or punched.

At first, football was played only on feast days and holidays. At other times, men's favourite sport was archery. They spent many hours on village greens, practising shooting with bows and arrows.

The kings of England were glad about this. They wanted every man to be a good archer, so that he could fight well in times of war.

But, as football became more popular, men began to play matches on the village green instead of practising archery. Then the kings were afraid the men would become poor archers.

King Edward III, King Richard II, King Henry IV and Queen Elizabeth, all passed laws forbidding men to play football.

Men who were found playing football were made to pay fines of money, or they were sent to prison. Yet even these laws did not stop men playing football.

The matches held on holidays grew bigger and bigger. The game was sometimes called hurling. The ball was passed by hand and carried in the hand, as well as being kicked. Often there were scrums.

By 1800 the game was a little more like the game of football that we know to-day. The same number of men played on each side.

The goals were eighty or one hundred yards apart. They were just two sticks driven into the ground, two or three feet apart. There was no crossbar. The first team to drive the ball through the opponent's goal was the winner.

The games were still so rough that a Frenchman watching one game could not believe that the men were playing a game. He said that, if this was what Englishmen called playing, he would not like to see them fighting.

When football was first played by men it was a very rough game. About 1800 the game began to be played in some boys' schools. Then it was not quite so rough, but it was very different from the games played in schools nowadays.

All the schools did not have the same rules. Each school made up rules of football to suit itself.

There was only one rule on which all the schools agreed. It was that the ball must never be carried, or passed by hand, towards the opponent's goal.

One famous school which played football was called Rugby School. In 1823, one of the boys at this school was called William Webb Ellis.

One day, during a game of football, Ellis picked up the ball and ran with it towards his opponent's goal. At first everyone was very angry with him.

But later it was agreed that, if a boy made a fair catch, he could run with the ball. Later still a boy was allowed to run with the ball if he caught it on the bound. Finally, running with the ball was allowed at any time.

William Webb Ellis, the boy who had first run with the ball, became a hero. A notice telling how Ellis first took the ball in his arms and ran with it, was fixed on the wall around Rugby School.

After 1823 there began to be two sorts of football, just as there are to-day. Those schools which allowed their boys to run with the ball, played Rugby Football.

Some schools would still not allow their players to run with the ball or to handle it. This sort of football we now call Soccer.

THIS STONE
COMMEMORATES THE EXPLOIT OF
WILLIAM WEBB ELLIS
WHO WITH A FINE DISREGARD FOR THE RULES OF FOOTBALL
AS PLAYED IN HIS TIME
FIRST TOOK THE BALL IN HIS ARMS AND RAN WITH IT
THUS ORIGINATING THE DISTINCTIVE FEATURE OF
THE RUGBY GAME
A.D. 1823

At this time, it was not possible to have football matches between one school and another, because each school had different rules.

Later however, boys who had left school began to wish that they could play in matches once more. So the first Football Clubs grew up.

In 1850 there were quite a number of Football Clubs. Each club drew up its own rules at a special meeting. The rules were not the same for every club. However, they all agreed that a team should be made up of twenty players. They also agreed on what was meant by offside.

In 1863 the first set of rules for all Football Clubs was published. A team was made up of eleven players, but their positions were different from nowadays. There was one goalkeeper, one full-back, one half-back and eight forwards.

The forwards did not make up a forward line as they do now. They used to run up and down the field in a pack and they did very little passing. Instead, they dribbled and charged. Mostly they charged the goalkeeper out of the way of the ball.

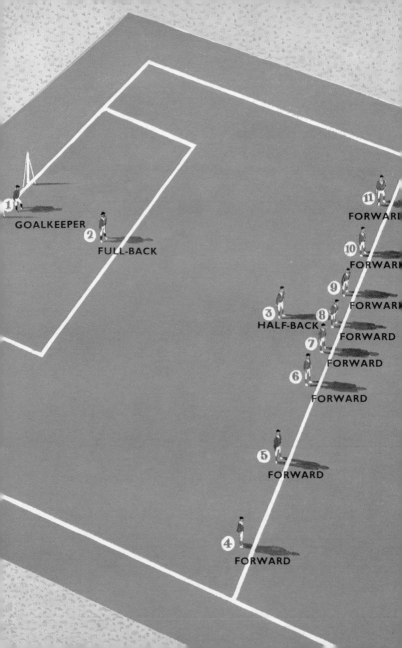

During the next ten or twenty years the positions of the members of a football team changed. It became more usual for a team to be made up of a goalkeeper, two full-backs, two half-backs, and six forwards.

By about 1883 most teams had turned another forward into a half-back. In this way we came to have the positions in a football team as they are to-day, with a goalkeeper, two full-backs, three half-backs and five forwards.

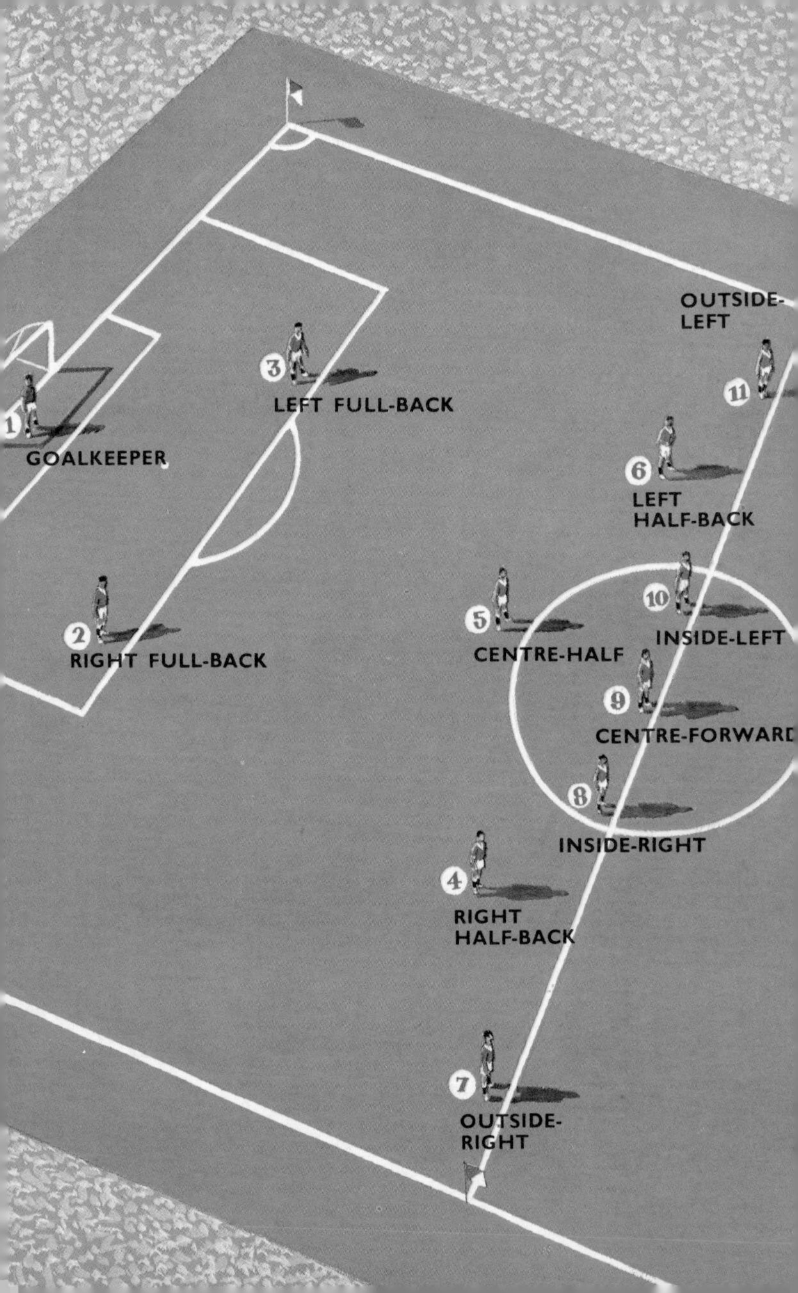

OUTSIDE-LEFT

3 LEFT FULL-BACK

1 GOALKEEPER

6 LEFT HALF-BACK

11

5 CENTRE-HALF

10 INSIDE-LEFT

2 RIGHT FULL-BACK

9 CENTRE-FORWARD

8 INSIDE-RIGHT

4 RIGHT HALF-BACK

7 OUTSIDE-RIGHT

The first teams to belong to the Football Association wore very different clothes from nowadays.

The players wore knickerbockers which were fastened down below their knees. Their stockings were very long and were pulled up over the bottoms of their knickerbockers. Their boots were just ordinary boots with two or three crossbars of leather fixed to the soles and one crossbar on each heel.

Most of the players had moustaches and many had beards. Generally they all wore caps, but sometimes a player wore a top hat.

Nowadays footballers wear fewer clothes and they are much more comfortable.

A footballer wears a shirt or jersey and shorts. His stockings come to just below his knees. Underneath his stockings he wears shin guards. These are to prevent him getting hurt, because a kick on the shin can be very painful. A footballer wears special football boots with studs on the soles. These prevent him slipping when the ground is soft.

The goalkeeper usually wears a thick jersey, which is a different colour from the shirts of the rest of the men in his team.

At first, when a player had to throw the ball in from touch, he threw it with one hand. Footballers soon became too good at this. A man could throw the ball into the goal-mouth from forty or fifty yards.

Then the rule was changed, so that two hands must be used to throw in the ball. Players soon became very good at this, too.

Finally the rule was made that the player must stand still and the ball must be thrown with two hands from above the head.

At the time when the goal-posts only had a tape stretched between them, there were many arguments as to whether a goal had really been scored or not. So in 1883 a wooden crossbar was placed on top of the goal-posts, instead of the tape.

Yet there were still many other quarrels during matches. At this time there were no linesmen. Each team had its own umpire. A referee was only used when the two umpires could not agree.

After 1891 the umpires became linesmen and the referee controlled the game, as he does nowadays.

As the game of football became more and more popular in this country, it began to spread to other countries. Now it is played nearly all over the world.

In 1930 the first World Cup tournament was played. Now it takes place regularly. Both amateur and professional teams can take part in this competition for the World Cup.

In India, Pakistan and a number of other countries, some of the players wear no boots. Their feet are so hard and strong that the men kick the ball with their bare feet.

When the Football League was first begun in 1888, it was made up of twelve football clubs. Now the Football League has over eighty teams, which are divided into four Divisions.

At the end of every season the first two clubs in the Second Division are promoted to the First Division. At the same time the lowest two teams in the First Division are relegated to the Second Division. Teams in other Divisions are promoted and relegated in the same way.

Every Saturday about one million people watch Football League matches. As many as eighty thousand or one hundred thousand people may watch one match.

As well as watching matches at football grounds, many other people listen to accounts of the matches on the radio. Some of the big matches are televised. They are shown on television on Saturday evenings, so that people who could not get to the match can still enjoy the game.

On both radio and television the results of the Football League games are announced every Saturday evening.

Every Saturday evening too, sporting papers are published, which give all the results and accounts of the matches.

The results of football matches are used in football pool competitions. Every week, thousands of people fill in football pool coupons. They try to guess which matches will be won and which will be drawn.

Football pool coupons make a great deal of work for postmen, who deliver them to houses on Mondays and Tuesdays. Then all the completed coupons are posted on Thursdays and Fridays.

On Saturdays, people check the football results to see if they have been lucky with their football pool coupons. Those who guess correctly win large sums of money.

The F.A. Cup competition, which is now so famous, was first begun in 1871. It is a knock-out competition. The winning team is given a large silver cup which it keeps for a year.

In 1895, the F.A. Cup was won by Aston Villa. When the team took the cup back to Birmingham, it was placed in the window of a Birmingham shop, so that everyone could see it.

During one night the cup was stolen from the shop window. It was never discovered who had taken it, so a new F.A. Cup had to be made.

Soon there were so many professional clubs that they always won the F.A. Cup from the amateur clubs. So the Football Association began another competition with another F.A. Cup, just for amateur clubs.

The Football Association is now so large that it is made up of more than sixty thousand clubs. This means that there are more than a million players.

There are usually large crowds at cup-tie matches. Many of the spectators wear rosettes, made in the colours of the team they support. Some of them carry bells and rattles, to make a noise at the match.

Every footballer longs to play in the final of the F.A. Cup at Wembley.

The Queen, or some member of the Royal Family, usually comes to the Cup Final at Wembley. At the end of the match, the Queen presents a cup to the captain of the winning team. Then she gives a medal to every member of the two teams. It is a wonderful moment for them.

The men in the winning team often carry their captain to the dressing room, on their shoulders, while he holds the F.A. Cup high above his head.

First Division League Champions
1950-1970

1949 - 1950   Portsmouth

1950 - 1951   Tottenham Hotspur

1951 - 1952   Manchester United

1952 - 1953   Arsenal

1953 - 1954   Wolverhampton Wanderers

1954 - 1955   Chelsea

1955 - 1956   Manchester United

1956 - 1957   Manchester United

1957 - 1958   Wolverhampton Wanderers

1958 - 1959   Wolverhampton Wanderers

1959 - 1960   Burnley

1960 - 1961   Tottenham Hotspur*

1961 - 1962   Ipswich Town

1962 - 1963   Everton

1963 - 1964   Liverpool

1964 - 1965   Manchester United

1965 - 1966   Liverpool

1966 - 1967   Manchester United

1967 - 1968   Manchester City

1968 - 1969   Leeds United

1969 - 1970   Everton

* *Double Event — League and Cup in same season*